HERSHEY'S® Chocolate
COOKBOOK

Ideals Publishing Corp.
Nashville, Tennessee

Introduction

Hershey Foods Corporation is world famous for its contribution to the wonderful world of chocolate. A tremendous variety of eating and baking products have made Hershey a household name for generations. Within these pages you will find an outstanding selection of recipes using Hershey's many superb baking products.

Contents

ISBN 0-8249-3082-7

The Hershey Logo is a Trademark of Hershey Foods Corporation, Ideals Publishing Corporation, Licensee.

Copyright © MCMLXXXII by
Hershey Foods Corporation.
All rights reserved.
Printed and bound in the
United States of America.

Associate Editor
and Food Stylist
Susan Noland

Published by Ideals Publishing Corporation.
Nelson Place at Elm Hill Pike
Nashville, Tennessee

Cover Recipes:
Basic Cookie Mix Variations:
    Cherry Chocolate Chip Cookies, 6
    Pinwheels, 6
    Peanutty Chewy Bars, 6

Chocolate and Cocoa Basics

Storage of Chocolate Products

Since chocolate contains cocoa butter, temperatures of 78°F and above cause chocolate to melt and cocoa butter to rise to the surface, forming a gray discoloration known as "cocoa butter bloom." "Sugar bloom" may occur when condensation forms on the surface of semi-sweet or milk chocolate, causing sugar to dissolve and rise to the surface. In both cases, the quality and flavor of the chocolate is not affected. Upon melting, the chocolate regains its original color. Chocolate products generally stay fresh well over a year when stored correctly. To avoid bloom, store chocolate in a cool, dry place where the temperature is about 70°F Chocolate can be refrigerated during hot, humid weather, but in some instances it may "bloom" when brought to room temperature.

Hershey's Baking Chocolate should be stored at room temperature but can be refrigerated during hot weather because it contains no sugar and will not develop sugar bloom. Hershey's Cocoa, Instant and Hot Cocoa Mix keep very well when stored at room temperature in tightly sealed containers. Store opened cans of Hershey's Chocolate Flavored Syrup and Hershey's Fudge Topping in refrigerator.

Melting Hints

1. Break or cut chocolate into 1-inch pieces prior to placing in top of a double boiler.
2. Melt milk chocolate in top of double boiler over warm water.
3. Melt semi-sweet chocolate in top of a double boiler over hot, not boiling, water.
4. Melt unsweetened baking chocolate in top of a double boiler over simmering water.
5. Melt peanut butter chips in the top of a double boiler over hot, not boiling, water. If melted chips become grainy or too thick, add 1 tablespoon shortening or vegetable oil to each 6 ounces of chips; stir to blend. Return to heat (over hot water) if necessary.
6. Thoroughly wash and dry double boiler after each use. Residue will affect taste of chocolate.
7. Regulate heat carefully! Chocolate scorches easily!

Garnish with Chocolate

Alleghetti Frosting (sometimes called Shadow Icing) is an easy way to dress up plain frosting. In a small saucepan combine 1 square (1 ounce) unsweetened chocolate and ½ teaspoon shortening. Heat over low heat, stirring constantly. Drizzle melted chocolate from a teaspoon around the edge of the cake to form "icicles."

Curls: Draw blade of vegetable parer over smooth side of a slightly warm block of unsweetened baking chocolate or a dark, sweet chocolate bar.

Cutouts: Melt 4 ounces semi-sweet and 1 ounce unsweetened chocolate in the top of a double boiler over boiling water. Remove from heat, let cool 5 minutes, and stir with a wooden spoon until pan is cool to your touch.

Line cookie sheet with waxed paper and spread chocolate 3⁄16 inch thick. Let cool until almost set. Press designs into chocolate, using cookie cutters. Peel paper from back of shape. Store on waxed paper in refrigerator.

Leaves: Gather 20 to 25 medium-size leaves with stems (English ivy, elm, dogwood). Wash and dry thoroughly. Melt 1 cup semi-sweet chocolate chips in top of double boiler over hot, not boiling, water. Remove from heat; keep over warm water. Carefully brush a thin layer (about ⅛ inch thick) of chocolate on underside of leaf. Chocolate and leaf will separate more easily if edges are not covered. Place coated leaves on wire rack until firm; chill if necessary. Carefully peel leaf from coating; store in cool place or refrigerator.

Tempering Hershey Products for Coating Candies

Have you ever wondered why commercially made chocolate-coated candy stays so glossy and firm at room temperature? It is because of a process called tempering. Tempering is achieved by heating and cooling chocolate to specific temperatures, causing cocoa butter crystal formation so that the chocolate coating will stay firm and glossy without the addition of wax or refrigeration of the coated candy. Although Hershey Chocolate is tempered during manufacturing, melting it destroys this temper; thus this process must be repeated by the consumer.

Carefully read all tips and instructions before beginning. Set aside about 2 to 3 hours to complete the process. The most important thing to remember is that the process (temperature changes) must happen evenly and slowly, with constant stirring. *It cannot be rushed.* Do not try to temper chocolate and coat candy on a humid day. Humidity, steam, wet pans, or utensils cause chocolate to thicken, tighten and become grainy. Even a few drops of water can cause problems, so make sure all utensils are dry before beginning.

Candies coated with chocolate that is *not* tempered will probably have a somewhat sticky coating that will "bloom." Bloom is white or gray spots or streaks caused by separation of the sugar or fat particles from the chocolate. Chocolate that has bloom is not harmful and does not taste different, but may look unappetizing.

Chocolate and Cocoa Basics

Tempering Instructions

1. Melt proper amount of chocolate and vegetable shortening in a small bowl set in a pan of very warm water. Make sure water level is 2 to 3 inches below rim of bowl. (Water temperature should not be above 120°F).
2. Heat chocolate to 108°F, stirring constantly with rubber spatula; scrape down sides and bottom of bowl frequently so that the chocolate is evenly and uniformly heated.
3. When chocolate reaches 108°F, remove bowl from pan of water. Stir frequently until chocolate cools to 85°F. Continue stirring and scraping bowl constantly until chocolate cools to 80°F.
4. Keep chocolate at 80°F, stirring constantly, for 10 minutes. This is important because it develops the crystals necessary for gloss. It may be necessary to briefly set bowl in warm water to maintain temperature.
5. Rewarm chocolate in pan of warm water to 86°F; hold at that temperature for 5 minutes before dipping.
6. *Important:* Keep chocolate at 86°F during entire dipping process. If temperature at this point goes below 84°, the entire tempering process must be repeated from Step #2.
7. Centers must be removed from refrigerator and allowed to reach room temperature before coating. (Dipping chilled centers may result in cracked coating and/or bloom on the coating.)
8. Dip room temperature centers or confections completely in tempered, melted chocolate. Dip one at a time using fork, fondue fork, or hat pin. Gently tap fork on side of bowl to remove excess chocolate. Invert onto waxed paper-covered tray; swirl small amount of coating over utensil marks.
9. Chill coated candies a maximum of 15 minutes in refrigerator to help coating harden. Remove promptly or bloom may occur.
10. Store coated candies at room temperature (60°-75°F), but keep them well covered.

Important Tips for Making Candy

1. The process is not difficult, but it does take time. Remember that "practice makes perfect." It becomes easier each time you do it.
2. It is critical that you do not try to rush the process or skip steps. Key words are slowly, evenly, and uniformly.
3. Use a candy thermometer which registers from 70°F to 110°F. Most will not work since they do not register below 100°F; laboratory thermometers do register temperatures in the appropriate range. The thermometer is critical to the process; you will not get good results without it.

   Test thermometer for accuracy by placing it in a pan of boiling water. An accurate thermometer will register 212°F at sea level. Add or subtract degrees from cooking temperatures in recipes according to the thermometer reading.

   To get an accurate reading, be sure that your candy thermometer is standing upright and that the bulb is covered by liquid. The bulb should not be resting on the bottom of the pan.
4. The chocolate mixture should be fluid at 108°F. If chocolate becomes tight or grainy due to humidity, stir in a small amount of solid vegetable shortening, one teaspoonful at a time, until chocolate is smooth and fluid again. At this point, retemper chocolate.
5. Use Step #4 only as an emergency measure. Do not purposely try to extend chocolate coatings with extra fat and/or water. This will ruin your coating.
6. Constant scraping and stirring as stated in the instructions will help insure success and is necessary for proper crystal formation.
7. Use solid vegetable shortening as directed, *not* butter or margarine. Butter and margarine contain moisture that will cause chocolate to tighten and become grainy.

Temperatures and Tests for Syrup and Candies

Test of Doneness	Final Temperature of Syrup at Sea Level*	Description of Test
Thread	230 to 234°F	Syrup spins a 2-inch thread when dropped from fork or spoon.
Soft ball	234 to 240°F	Syrup, when dropped into very cold water, forms a soft ball which flattens on removal from water.
Firm ball	244 to 248°F	Syrup, when dropped into very cold water, forms a firm ball which does not flatten on removal from water.
Hard ball	250 to 266°F	Syrup, when dropped into very cold water, forms a ball which is hard enough to hold its shape, yet plastic.
Soft crack	270 to 290°F	Syrup, when dropped into very cold water, separates into threads which are hard but not brittle.
Hard crack	300 to 310°F	Syrup, when dropped into very cold water, separates into threads which are hard and brittle.

*For each 500 feet of elevation, cook the syrup to a temperature 1° lower than temperature called for at sea level.

Handbook for Food Preparation Eighth Edition © 1980
American Home Economics Association

Glossary of Chocolate and Cocoa Products

Artificial or Synthetic Chocolate: An imitation product which contains no cocoa bean derived ingredients. In the extreme, it can mean no milk or sugar either—all replacement ingredients. Hershey produces no artificial chocolate.

Bitter Chocolate: (Commonly referred to as unsweetened, baking, or cooking chocolate). Chocolate liquor which has been cooled and molded, usually in blocks.

Cacao (cocoa) Beans: The source of cocoa and chocolate, cacao beans are the fruit of the cacao tree, which grows only 20° north or south of the equator and mainly in West Africa and Latin America.

Cacao Nibs: The "meat" of the cacao bean. After the beans are cleaned and roasted at controlled temperatures to bring out the full flavor and aroma, the outer shells are removed, leaving the nibs.

Chocolate: Although legally this means unsweetened (bitter) chocolate or chocolate liquor (see below), common usage implies milk chocolate, semi-sweet chocolate, and sweet chocolate.

Chocolate Flavored: This term is used for food products flavored with cocoa and/or chocolate liquor, but not containing enough of these substances to be called chocolate as defined by the Standards of Identity (see below).

Chocolate Flavored Syrup: Commonly referred to as chocolate syrup. A combination, in varying proportions, of chocolate liquor or cocoa, sugar, water, salt, and sometimes other flavorings such as vanilla.

Chocolate Liquor: Base material of all chocolate products. The nibs, which contain more than 50% cocoa butter, are ground by a process which generates enough heat to liquify the cocoa butter and form chocolate liquor. Chocolate liquor has no alcoholic content.

Cocoa Butter: A vegetable fat extracted from chocolate liquor by "pressing" at high pressure. The distinctive melting properties of cocoa butter give chocolate products their satisfying texture.

Cocoa Powder: The dry substance of chocolate liquor that remains after most of the cocoa butter has been extracted.

Cocoa Powder (Dutch Process): Cocoa powder from nibs or chocolate liquor which has been treated with alkali to neutralize the natural acids. Dutch Process cocoa is darker, and the flavor slightly different from that of the so-called natural cocoa.

Compound Chocolate: A term used in the chocolate industry for chocolate-like products in which most or all of the cocoa butter has been removed and replaced by another vegetable fat. Frequently referred to as "white chocolate" or confectioners' coating by consumers, it is available in dark, white, or pastel colors.

Milk Chocolate: A combination of chocolate liquor, added cocoa butter, sugar, and milk or cream. It must contain at least 10% chocolate liquor. It may also contain optional ingredients.

Premelted Baking Chocolate-Type Product: A mixture of unsweetened cocoa and vegetable oil in foil or plastic envelopes.

Semi-Sweet Chocolate: A combination of chocolate liquor, added cocoa butter, and sugar. It must contain at least 35% chocolate liquor. Most commonly known in the form of semi-sweet chocolate chips.

Sweet (Dark) Chocolate: A combination of chocolate liquor, added cocoa butter, and sugar. It must contain at least 15% chocolate liquor and has a higher proportion of sugar than semi-sweet chocolate.

Standards of Identity: A rigid set of identifications, as established by the Food and Drug Administration (FDA), which designates for each chocolate and cocoa product the percentage of key ingredients that must be present in order for them to bear the name of such product.

Substitutions

For Baking Chocolate: 3 tablespoons cocoa plus 1 tablespoon shortening or oil equals 1 square (1 ounce) baking chocolate.

For Premelted Unsweetened Chocolate: 3 tablespoons cocoa plus 1 tablespoon oil or melted shortening equals 1 envelope (1 ounce) pre-melted unsweetened chocolate.

For Semi-sweet Chocolate: 6 tablespoons cocoa plus 7 tablespoons sugar plus ¼ cup shortening equals 1 6-ounce package (1 cup) semi-sweet chocolate chips or 6 squares (1 ounce each) semi-sweet chocolate.

For Sweet Cooking Chocolate: 3 tablespoons cocoa plus 4½ tablespoons sugar plus 2⅔ tablespoons shortening equals 1 4-ounce bar sweet cooking chocolate.

Note: In these substitutions, don't use butter or margarine. They contain a slight amount of water, which could cause ingredients to separate.

There are three easy ways to use cocoa in recipes that originally called for another chocolate product:

1. Combine cocoa (and sugar) with the dry ingredients. Add the extra shortening with the shortening called for in the recipe.
2. Melt the extra shortening. Remove from heat and blend in cocoa. If you're using oil, merely blend oil and cocoa. Add mixture to the recipe as you would premelted unsweetened chocolate.
3. For extra cocoa flavor and color, add the extra shortening with the shortening called for in the recipe. Mix cocoa and part of the water called for in the recipe into a smooth paste. Add to the creamed mixture.

Cookies

Basic Cookie Mix

Makes approximately 11 cups.

    5 cups unsifted all-purpose flour
    2 cups granulated sugar
    1 cup packed brown sugar
    2 tablespoons baking powder
    1 tablespoon salt
    1 cup shortening
    ½ cup butter

Combine flour, granulated sugar, brown sugar, baking powder, and salt in a large bowl. (You can use an electric mixer on slow speed for mixing.) Add shortening and butter; cut in with pastry blender or hands until mixture resembles coarse cornmeal. Store in an airtight container in refrigerator.

Note: After refrigeration, measure amount of mix needed; bring to room temperature for easier blending.

Peanutty Chewy Bars

Makes 24.

    2½ cups Basic Cookie Mix (Recipe above)
    ⅓ cup Hershey's Cocoa
    ⅓ cup granulated sugar
    2 eggs, lightly beaten
    1 cup Reese's Peanut Butter Chips
    1⅓ cups (14-ounce can) sweetened condensed milk
    1 cup flaked coconut

Combine cookie mix, cocoa, sugar, and eggs in a large bowl; blend well. Spread in a greased 13 x 9 x 2-inch baking pan. Bake at 350° for 8 to 10 minutes or until mixture is set. Remove from oven. Sprinkle peanut butter chips over top. Drizzle sweetened condensed milk evenly over chips; top with coconut. Return to oven; bake for 20 to 25 minutes or until lightly browned on top. Cool in pan. Cut into bars.

Cherry Chocolate Chip Cookies

Makes approximately 2½ dozen.

    2½ cups Basic Cookie Mix (Recipe above)
    ¼ cup sour cream
    ¼ cup finely chopped, well-drained maraschino cherries
    1 cup Hershey's Semi-Sweet Chocolate Chips
    1 cup chopped nuts
    30 maraschino cherry halves, well drained

Stir together cookie mix, sour cream, cherries, and chocolate chips in a large bowl. Shape into 1-inch balls; roll in nuts. Place on a greased cookie sheet. Garnish each with a cherry half. Bake at 375° for 8 to 10 minutes. Remove from cookie sheet; cool on a wire rack.

Sugar Cookies

Makes approximately 2 dozen.

    3 cups Basic Cookie Mix (Recipe on this page)
    1 egg plus 1 egg yolk, lightly beaten
    1 teaspoon vanilla
    1 egg white, lightly beaten

Combine cookie mix, egg, egg yolk, and vanilla in a small bowl. Cover; chill until firm, about 3 hours. Divide dough in half; roll each half to desired thickness on a lightly floured surface. Cut into desired shapes; brush with egg white. Place on a greased cookie sheet. Bake at 375° for 8 to 10 minutes or until lightly browned. (Cookies spread considerably during baking.) Remove from cookie sheet. Cool on a wire rack.

Variations

Surprise Cookies Makes approximately 1½ dozen: Roll dough on a lightly floured surface to ¼ inch thick. Cut into 2½-inch circles. Place on a greased cookie sheet. Break a ½ pound Hershey's Milk Chocolate Bar into squares. Place a square in the center of each circle; place another circle on top. Seal edges with the tines of a fork. (Reserve remaining chocolate squares for Pinwheels below.) Bake at 375° for 10 to 12 minutes. Remove from cookie sheet. Cool on a wire rack.

Pinwheels Makes approximately 3 dozen: Melt 4 ounces of a Hershey's Milk Chocolate Bar or remaining squares from the Surprise Cookies above; cool. Divide dough in half; roll out each half into a rectangle on a lightly floured surface to ¼-inch thickness. Spread with melted chocolate; roll up dough from the long side. Wrap dough in plastic; refrigerate until well chilled. Cut into ¼-inch slices. Place on a greased cookie sheet. Bake at 375° for 8 to 10 minutes. Remove from cookie sheet. Cool on a wire rack.

Basic Cookie Mix Variations: Cherry Chocolate Chip Cookies, above
Pinwheels, above
Peanutty Chewy Bars, above

Cookies

Peanut Blossoms

Makes approximately 4 dozen.

- ½ cup shortening
- ¾ cup peanut butter
- ⅓ cup granulated sugar
- ⅓ cup packed brown sugar
- 1 egg
- 2 tablespoons milk
- 1 teaspoon vanilla
- 1½ cups unsifted all-purpose flour
- 1 teaspoon baking soda
- ½ teaspoon salt
- Granulated sugar
- 1 9-ounce package (about 54) Hershey's Milk Chocolate Kisses

Cream shortening and peanut butter in large bowl. Blend in granulated sugar and brown sugar. Add egg, milk, and vanilla; beat well. In a separate bowl combine flour, baking soda, and salt. Gradually add flour mixture to creamed mixture; blend thoroughly. Shape dough into 1-inch balls. Roll in granulated sugar. Place on an ungreased cookie sheet. Bake at 375° for 10 to 12 minutes. Remove from oven. Immediately place an *unwrapped* Kiss on top of each cookie, pressing down so that cookie cracks around the edges. Remove from cookie sheet. Cool on a wire rack.

Crunchy Oatmeal Peanut Butter Chip Cookies

Makes approximately 5 dozen.

- ¾ cup butter *or* margarine
- 1 cup packed brown sugar
- ½ cup granulated sugar
- 1 egg
- 1 teaspoon vanilla
- 1 cup unsifted all-purpose flour
- ½ teaspoon baking soda
- ½ teaspoon salt
- ¼ cup milk
- 2½ cups quick-cooking rolled oats
- 2 cups (12-ounce package) Reese's Peanut Butter Chips

Cream butter *or* margarine, brown sugar, granulated sugar, egg, and vanilla in large bowl. In a separate bowl combine flour, baking soda, and salt. Alternately beat in flour mixture and milk to creamed mixture. Stir in oats and peanut butter chips. Drop by teaspoonfuls onto a greased cookie sheet. Bake at 375° for 10 to 12 minutes or until light brown. Remove from cookie sheet. Cool on a wire rack.

Double Peanut Butter Cookies

Makes approximately 3½ dozen.

- ¼ cup butter *or* margarine
- ¼ cup shortening
- ½ cup peanut butter
- ½ cup granulated sugar
- ½ cup packed brown sugar
- 1 egg
- 1¼ cups unsifted all-purpose flour
- ¾ teaspoon baking soda
- ½ teaspoon baking powder
- ¼ teaspoon salt
- 2 cups (12-ounce package) Reese's Peanut Butter Chips

Cream butter *or* margarine, shortening, peanut butter, sugar, brown sugar, and egg in a large bowl. Blend in flour, baking soda, baking powder, and salt. Stir in peanut butter chips. Shape into 1-inch balls. Place on an ungreased cookie sheet. Flatten in a criss-cross pattern with a fork dipped in sugar. Bake at 375° for 10 to 12 minutes or until set. Cool several minutes before removing from cookie sheet onto a wire rack.

Macaroon Kiss Cookies

Makes approximately 4½ dozen.

- ⅓ cup butter *or* margarine
- 1 3-ounce package cream cheese
- ¾ cup granulated sugar
- 1 egg yolk
- 2 teaspoons almond extract
- 2 teaspoons brandy
- 1¼ cups unsifted all-purpose flour
- 2 teaspoons baking powder
- ¼ teaspoon salt
- 5 cups (14-ounce package) flaked coconut
- 1 9-ounce package (about 54) Hershey's Milk Chocolate Kisses

Cream butter *or* margarine, cream cheese, and sugar in a large bowl. Add egg yolk, almond extract, and brandy; beat well. In a separate bowl, combine flour, baking powder, and salt. Gradually add flour mixture to creamed mixture; blend well. Stir in 3 cups of the flaked coconut. Chill dough about 1 hour. Shape dough into 1-inch balls. Roll balls in the remaining 2 cups coconut. Place on an ungreased cookie sheet; flatten with a fork. Bake at 350° for 12 to 15 minutes or until lightly browned on the bottoms. Remove from oven. Press an *unwrapped* Kiss into the center of each cookie; return to oven for 15 seconds. Carefully remove cookies from cookie sheet.

Chocolate Drop Cookies

Makes approximately 4 dozen.

- ⅔ cup butter *or* margarine, softened
- 1 cup granulated sugar
- 1½ teaspoons vanilla
- 1 egg
- 1½ cups unsifted all-purpose flour
- ½ cup Hershey's Cocoa
- ½ teaspoon baking soda
- ¼ teaspoon salt
- ⅓ cup buttermilk *or* sour milk*

Cream butter *or* margarine and granulated sugar in large bowl. Blend in vanilla and egg. In a separate bowl combine flour, cocoa, baking soda, and salt. Alternately add flour mixture and buttermilk *or* sour milk to creamed mixture. Drop by teaspoonfuls 2 inches apart onto a lightly greased cookie sheet. Bake at 350° for 7 to 9 minutes. Remove from cookie sheet. Cool on a wire rack. Frost, if desired.

To Sour Milk: Use 1 teaspoon vinegar plus milk to equal ⅓ cup.

Chocolate Rum Balls

Makes approximately 4 dozen.

- 3¼ cups (12-ounce package) crushed vanilla wafers
- ¾ cup confectioners' sugar
- ¼ cup Hershey's Cocoa
- 1½ cups chopped nuts
- 3 tablespoons light corn syrup
- ½ cup rum *or* ½ cup orange juice plus 1 teaspoon grated orange peel
  Confectioners' sugar

Combine vanilla wafer crumbs, confectioners' sugar, cocoa, and nuts in a large bowl. Blend in corn syrup, rum *or* orange juice, and grated peel. Shape into 1-inch balls. Roll in confectioners' sugar. Store in an airtight container several days to develop flavor. Roll again in confectioners' sugar before serving.

Thumbprint Kiss Cookies

Makes approximately 2 dozen.

- 1 egg, lightly beaten
- 1 teaspoon vanilla
- 2½ cups Chocolate Cookie Mix (Recipe on page 12)
  Chopped nuts
- 24 Hershey's Milk Chocolate Kisses
  Vanilla Frosting (Recipe on page 12)

Combine first three ingredients in a bowl; blend well. Form into 1-inch balls. Roll each in chopped nuts. Place on a cookie sheet. Press down center of each with your thumb. Bake at 375° for 8 to 10 minutes. Remove from oven. Place a dot of Vanilla Frosting in center of each cookie. Immediately press an *unwrapped* Kiss into frosting. Remove from cookie sheet; cool on a wire rack.

Holiday Chocolate Drop Cookies

Makes approximately 3 dozen.

- ½ cup butter *or* margarine
- 1¼ cups packed brown sugar
- 2 eggs
- ¼ cup Hershey's Cocoa
- 1½ cups unsifted all-purpose flour
- ½ teaspoon baking soda
- ¼ teaspoon salt
- 1 teaspoon vanilla
- ½ cup snipped dates
- 1 cup raisins
- ½ cup chopped walnuts

Cream butter *or* margarine and sugar in a large bowl. Add eggs; beat well. In a separate bowl combine cocoa, flour, baking soda, and salt. Blend flour mixture into creamed mixture. Add vanilla, dates, raisins, and walnuts. Chill for 30 minutes. Drop by teaspoonfuls onto a lightly greased cookie sheet. Bake at 350° for 8 to 10 minutes or until set. Remove from cookie sheet. Cool on a wire rack.

Peanut Butter Chip Cookies

Makes approximately 5 dozen.

- 1 cup shortening *or* ¾ cup butter *or* margarine
- 1 cup granulated sugar
- ½ cup packed light brown sugar
- 1 teaspoon vanilla
- 2 eggs
- 2 cups unsifted all-purpose flour
- 1 teaspoon baking soda
- 2 cups (12-ounce package) Reese's Peanut Butter Chips

Cream shortening *or* butter *or* margarine, granulated sugar, brown sugar, and vanilla in a large bowl. Add eggs; beat well. In a separate bowl combine flour and baking soda. Gradually add flour to creamed mixture; blend well. Stir in peanut butter chips. Drop by teaspoonfuls onto an ungreased cookie sheet. Bake at 350° for 10 to 12 minutes or until light brown. Cool slightly on cookie sheet before removing to a wire rack.

Hoot Owl Cookies

Makes approximately 2½ dozen.

- ¾ cup butter *or* margarine
- 1 cup packed brown sugar
- 1 egg
- 1½ teaspoons vanilla
- 2¼ cups unsifted all-purpose flour
- 2 teaspoons baking powder
- ½ teaspoon salt
- ⅓ cup Hershey's Cocoa
- ¼ teaspoon baking soda
- 1 tablespoon water
- ¼ cup Reese's Peanut Butter Chips
- ½ cup whole cashew nuts

Cream butter *or* margarine, brown sugar, egg, and vanilla in large bowl. In a separate bowl, combine flour, baking powder, and salt. Blend flour mixture into creamed mixture. Remove two-thirds of the dough to a floured surface. In small bowl combine cocoa and baking soda; add to remaining dough. Blend water into chocolate dough.

Roll half of the vanilla dough into a 10 x 4-inch rectangle. Shape half of chocolate dough into a roll 10 inches long; place in center of rectangle of vanilla dough. Mold sides of vanilla dough around roll of chocolate dough. Repeat shaping steps with remaining dough. Wrap in plastic wrap; chill at least 2 hours or overnight.

Cut dough into ⅛-inch thick slices; lay two slices together side-by-side on a greased cookie sheet. Pinch a corner of each slice to form ears. Place a peanut butter chip in the center of each slice for eyes; press a cashew nut between slices for a beak. Bake at 350° for 8 to 10 minutes or until set. Remove from cookie sheet; cool on rack.

Peanut Butter & Jelly Thumbprints

Makes approximately 5 dozen.

- 1 cup butter *or* margarine
- 1¾ cups packed brown sugar
- 2 eggs
- 2 teaspoons vanilla
- 3 cups unsifted all-purpose flour
- 1 teaspoon baking powder
- 1 teaspoon salt
- 2 cups (12-ounce package) Reese's Peanut Butter Chips
- 1½ cups quick-cooking rolled oats
- ¾ cup jelly *or* preserves (apple, grape, peach, etc.)

Cream butter *or* margarine and brown sugar in large bowl. Add eggs and vanilla; beat until light and fluffy. In a separate bowl combine flour, baking powder, and salt. Gradually add flour mixture to creamed mixture. Reserve ½ cup peanut butter chips. Stir in oats and 1½ cups peanut butter chips. Shape dough into 1-inch balls. Place balls on an ungreased cookie sheet. Press the center of each with your thumb to make a deep depression about 1 inch wide. Bake at 400° for 7 to 9 minutes or until lightly browned. Remove from cookie sheet. Cool on a wire rack. Fill center of each cookie with ½ teaspoon jelly *or* preserves; top with several of the reserved peanut butter chips.

No-Bake Peanut Butter Chip Cookies

Makes approximately 4 dozen.

- 2 cups (12-ounce package) Reese's Peanut Butter Chips
- 1 tablespoon shortening
- 5 cups cornflakes cereal, coarsely crushed
- 1 cup raisins

Melt peanut butter chips and shortening in top of a double boiler over hot, *not* boiling, water. Stir until smooth and creamy. Combine cereal, melted chips, and raisins; stir until cereal is coated. Drop by teaspoonfuls onto a waxed paper-lined cookie sheet. Cover and chill for 1 hour.

Hershey's Chocolate Chip Cookies

Makes approximately 6 dozen.

- 1 cup butter *or* margarine, softened
- ¾ cup packed brown sugar
- ¾ cup granulated sugar
- 2 eggs
- 1 teaspoon vanilla
- 2¼ cups unsifted all-purpose flour
- 1 teaspoon baking soda
- ½ teaspoon salt
- 1 cup chopped nuts
- 2 cups (12-ounce package) Hershey's Semi-Sweet Chocolate Chips

Cream butter *or* margarine, brown sugar, granulated sugar, eggs, and vanilla in a large bowl. In a separate bowl combine flour, baking soda, and salt. Blend into creamed mixture. Stir in nuts and chocolate chips. Drop by teaspoonfuls onto an ungreased cookie sheet. Bake at 375° for 8 to 10 minutes or until light brown. Cool slightly on cookie sheet before removing to a wire rack.

Cookies

Maple-Nut Chocolate Brownies

Makes 16.

2 eggs
1 cup granulated sugar
½ teaspoon vanilla
½ cup butter *or* margarine, melted
½ cup unsifted all-purpose flour
¼ teaspoon baking powder
¼ teaspoon salt
⅓ cup chopped nuts
¾ teaspoon maple flavoring
¼ cup Hershey's Cocoa
    Confectioners' sugar, optional

Beat eggs in small bowl. Gradually add sugar and vanilla. Blend in melted butter *or* margarine; beat well. In a separate bowl combine flour, baking powder, and salt. Gradually add to creamed mixture; blend thoroughly. Remove 1 cup of the batter; stir in chopped nuts and maple flavoring. Add cocoa to remaining batter; blend thoroughly. Spoon into a greased 8-inch square baking pan in 4 alternate rows, i.e. chocolate-maple-chocolate-maple. Use a rubber spatula or scraper to zigzag lightly through the batter, being careful not to blend too well. Bake at 350° for 35 to 40 minutes or until brownie begins to pull away from edges of pan. Cool in pan. Sprinkle lightly with confectioners' sugar, if desired. Cut into squares.

Chocolate Cookie Mix

Makes approximately 11 cups.

4 cups unsifted all-purpose flour
4 cups granulated sugar
1⅓ cups Hershey's Cocoa
2 teaspoons baking powder
1 teaspoon salt
1½ cups butter *or* margarine

Combine thoroughly flour, sugar, cocoa, baking powder, and salt in a large bowl. (An electric mixer on slow speed can be used for mixing.) Add butter *or* margarine; cut in with a pastry blender or with hands until mixture resembles coarse cornmeal. Store in an airtight container in refrigerator.

Note: After refrigeration, measure amount of mix needed; bring to room temperature for easier blending.

Chewy Chocolate Wafers

Makes approximately 3 dozen.

1 egg, lightly beaten
1 teaspoon vanilla
2½ cups Chocolate Cookie Mix (Recipe on this page)

Combine all ingredients in a bowl; blend well. Place on waxed paper. Shape into a log about 8 inches long. Wrap tightly in waxed paper. Refrigerate for 30 minutes. Reshape log to keep it round. Chill until firm. Slice ⅛ inch thick. Place on a lightly greased cookie sheet. Bake at 375° for 5 to 7 minutes or until set. Remove from cookie sheet. Cool on a wire rack. Frost with Vanilla Frosting, if desired.

Vanilla Frosting

1 cup confectioners' sugar
1 tablespoon shortening
1 to 2 tablespoons milk
½ teaspoon vanilla

Combine all ingredients in a small bowl. Beat until spreading consistency.

Brownies

Makes 16.

2 eggs
1 teaspoon vanilla
3 cups Chocolate Cookie Mix (Recipe on this page)
½ cup chopped nuts

Combine eggs and vanilla in a large bowl; beat lightly. Add cookie mix and chopped nuts. Stir until ingredients are well blended. Spoon into a greased, 8-inch square baking pan. Bake at 350° for 25 to 30 minutes or until brownie begins to pull away from sides of pan. (Do not overbake.) Cool in pan. Frost with Mint Frosting, if desired. Cut into bars.

Mint Frosting

1½ cups confectioners' sugar
2 tablespoons milk
1 tablespoon shortening
½ teaspoon vanilla
⅛ teaspoon pure mint *or* peppermint extract
2 or 3 drops green food color, optional

Combine all ingredients in the order listed in a small mixing bowl. Beat until spreading consistency. Additional sugar may be needed, if frosting is too thin.

Cinnamon Chocolate Chip Drops

Makes approximately 3 dozen.

- 3 cups Basic Cookie Mix (Recipe on page 6)
- 1 teaspoon cinnamon
- ¼ cup milk
- 1 egg, lightly beaten
- 1 cup Hershey's Semi-Sweet Chocolate Mini Chips
- ¾ cup chopped nuts

Combine all ingredients, except Mini Chips and nuts, in a large bowl; blend well. Stir in Mini Chips and nuts. Drop by teaspoonfuls onto a greased cookie sheet. Bake at 375° for 10 to 12 minutes. Remove from cookie sheet; cool on a wire rack.

Chocolate Cherry Drops

Makes approximately 4 dozen.

- ½ cup plus 2 tablespoons butter or margarine
- 1 cup granulated sugar
- 1 egg
- 1 teaspoon vanilla
- 1¼ cups unsifted all-purpose flour
- ¼ cup plus 2 tablespoons Hershey's Cocoa
- ½ teaspoon baking soda
- ½ teaspoon salt
- 1 cup chopped, well-drained maraschino cherries
- ½ cup chopped nuts
  Candied cherries or walnut pieces, optional

Cream butter or margarine and sugar in a large bowl. Add egg and vanilla; blend well. In a separate bowl combine flour, cocoa, baking soda, and salt. Blend flour mixture into creamed mixture. Stir in maraschino cherries and chopped nuts. Drop by rounded teaspoonfuls onto an ungreased cookie sheet. Garnish with candied cherries or walnut pieces, if desired. Bake at 350° for 10 to 12 minutes or until set. Remove from cookie sheet. Cool on a wire rack.

Chocolate Nut Drop Cookies

Makes approximately 2 dozen.

- 1 egg
- 1 tablespoon vegetable oil
- 1 teaspoon vanilla
- 2 cups Chocolate Cookie Mix (Recipe on page 12)
- ½ cup chopped nuts
  Maraschino cherries or walnut halves

Combine egg, oil, and vanilla in a bowl; beat until well blended. Add cookie mix and chopped nuts; blend well. Drop by teaspoonfuls onto a lightly greased cookie sheet. Top with a maraschino cherry or walnut half. Bake at 375° for 8 to 10 minutes or until set. Remove from cookie sheet; cool on a wire rack.

Peanut Butter Chip Chocolate Cookies

Makes approximately 5 dozen.

- 1 cup butter or margarine
- 1½ cups granulated sugar
- 2 eggs
- 2 teaspoons vanilla
- 2 cups unsifted all-purpose flour
- ⅔ cup Hershey's Cocoa
- ¾ teaspoon baking soda
- ½ teaspoon salt
- 2 cups (12-ounce package) Reese's Peanut Butter Chips

Cream butter or margarine, sugar, eggs, and vanilla in a large bowl. In a separate bowl combine flour, cocoa, baking soda, and salt. Blend into creamed mixture. Stir in peanut butter chips. Drop by teaspoonfuls onto an ungreased cookie sheet. (Alternate method: Chill until firm enough to handle. Shape into 1-inch balls. Place on an ungreased cookie sheet. Flatten slightly with a fork.) Bake at 350° for 8 to 10 minutes. Cool 1 minute on cookie sheet before removing to a wire rack.

Double Decker Brownies

Makes 16.

- 1 recipe Brownies (Recipe on page 12)
- 1 cup miniature marshmallows
- 1 cup Reese's Peanut Butter Chips
- 1 tablespoon shortening
- 1½ cups crisp rice cereal

Prepare recipe for Brownies, omitting nuts. Bake for 25 minutes. Remove from oven. Evenly sprinkle miniature marshmallows over brownies. Return to oven. Bake 5 additional minutes. Remove from oven. Cool in pan. Combine peanut butter chips and shortening in the top of a double boiler over hot, not boiling, water. Stir until melted. Add the rice cereal; stir until thoroughly coated. Spread over top of marshmallows. Cool until set. Cut into squares.

Cocoa Pinwheel Cookies

Makes approximately 3 dozen.

- ½ cup butter *or* margarine
- 1 3-ounce package cream cheese
- 1 cup granulated sugar
- 1 egg
- 1 teaspoon vanilla
- 1½ cups unsifted all-purpose flour
- ½ teaspoon baking powder
- ½ teaspoon salt
- ⅛ teaspoon baking soda
- ½ cup Hershey's Cocoa
- ¾ cup unsifted all-purpose flour

Cream butter *or* margarine, cream cheese, sugar, egg, and vanilla in large bowl. In a separate bowl combine 1½ cups flour, baking powder, salt, and baking soda. Gradually add flour mixture to creamed mixture; blend well. Divide dough in half. Blend cocoa into one half of the dough. Blend ¾ cup flour into remaining dough. Roll each portion into a 9-inch square. (If dough is too soft, chill for 15 minutes.) Place chocolate layer on top of vanilla; roll up jelly-roll style. Wrap tightly in waxed paper or plastic wrap. Chill at least 1 hour or overnight. Slice dough ¼-inch thick. Place on an ungreased cookie sheet. Bake at 350° for 12 to 15 minutes or until lightly browned. Remove from cookie sheet. Cool on a wire rack.

Ornament Cookies

Makes approximately 2 dozen.

- ½ cup butter *or* margarine
- ¾ cup granulated sugar
- 1 egg
- ¾ teaspoon pure mint *or* peppermint extract
- 1 tablespoon milk
- 1½ cups unsifted all-purpose flour
- ⅓ cup Hershey's Cocoa
- ½ teaspoon baking powder
- ⅛ teaspoon salt
- Red cinnamon candies, colored sprinkles, gumdrops, optional

Cream butter *or* margarine, sugar, egg, extract, and milk in a large bowl until light and fluffy. In a separate bowl stir together flour, cocoa, baking powder, and salt. Gradually add flour mixture to creamed mixture; blend well. Divide dough into quarters. Wrap tightly; chill 2 to 3 hours. Roll out dough, one-quarter at a time, to ⅛-inch thickness on a lightly floured cloth-covered board. Cut out half of the dough with a gingerbread boy or

girl cookie cutter, or use a star, bell, reindeer, Santa Claus, or other Christmas shapes; cut remaining dough into 3 x 2½-inch rectangles to resemble gift tags. Make a hole in the top of each cookie for hanging on the tree. Place cookies 1 inch apart on an ungreased cookie sheet. Use cinnamon candies to make buttons on gingerbread cookies and holly berries on gift tags. Bake at 325° for 8 to 10 minutes or until firm. Remove from cookie sheet; cool on a wire rack. Decorate cookies with Decorator Frosting and, if desired, colored sprinkles and gumdrops.

Decorator Frosting

- 2½ to 3 cups confectioners' sugar
- 2 egg whites
- ¼ teaspoon peppermint extract

Combine all ingredients in a small bowl. Increase speed to high and beat until mixture is very stiff.

Cocoa Press Cookies

Makes approximately 4½ dozen.

- 1 cup butter *or* margarine
- ⅔ cup granulated sugar
- 1 egg
- 1 teaspoon vanilla
- 2¼ cups unsifted all-purpose flour
- ⅓ cup Hershey's Cocoa
- ½ teaspoon salt

Cream butter *or* margarine, sugar, egg, and vanilla in large bowl. In a separate bowl combine flour, cocoa, and salt. Blend into creamed mixture. Fill cookie press with dough. Press cookies onto a cool, ungreased cookie sheet. Bake at 350° for 5 to 7 minutes or until set. Remove from cookie sheet. Cool on a wire rack.

Peanut Butter Chip Orange Bars

Makes 16.

- 2 cups Basic Cookie Mix (Recipe on page 6)
- ½ cup sour cream
- 2 teaspoons grated orange peel
- 1 cup Reese's Peanut Butter Chips
- 1 cup confectioners' sugar
- 1½ tablespoons orange juice

Combine cookie mix, sour cream, and orange peel in a small bowl. Stir in peanut butter chips. Spread in a greased 9-inch square baking pan. Bake at 350° for 20 to 25 minutes. Combine confectioners' sugar and orange juice; drizzle over cooled mixture. Cut into bars.

Cocoa Press Cookies, above
Ornament Cookies, above

Cookies

Deluxe Marbled Brownies

Makes approximately 2 dozen.

- **1 cup butter** *or* **margarine, softened**
- **2 cups granulated sugar**
- **4 eggs**
- **2 teaspoons vanilla**
- **1⅓ cups unsifted all-purpose flour**
- **¾ cup Hershey's Cocoa**
- **1 teaspoon baking powder**
- **½ teaspoon salt**
- **1 cup chopped nuts, optional**
- **⅓ cup butter** *or* **margarine**
- **2 3-ounce packages cream cheese, softened**
- **⅓ cup granulated sugar**
- **2 tablespoons unsifted all-purpose flour**
- **2 eggs**
- **¾ teaspoon vanilla**

Cream the 1 cup butter *or* margarine and 2 cups sugar in large bowl. Add 4 eggs, 1 at a time, beating well after each addition. Blend in 2 teaspoons vanilla. In a separate bowl combine 1⅓ cups flour, cocoa, baking powder, and salt. Gradually add flour mixture to creamed mixture; blend well. Stir in nuts, if desired. Spread half of the batter into a greased 13 x 9-inch baking pan.

Cream ⅓ cup butter *or* margarine and cream cheese in small bowl. Add ⅓ cup sugar and 2 tablespoons flour; blend well. Add 2 eggs and ¾ teaspoon vanilla; beat until smooth.

Spread cream cheese mixture over chocolate batter in pan. Carefully spread remaining chocolate batter over cream cheese mixture. Gently swirl with a spatula or knife for marbled effect. Bake at 350° for 40 to 50 minutes or until brownie begins to pull away from edges of pan. Cool in pan. Frost, if desired. Cut into squares.

Chocolate Brownies

Makes 16.

- **2 eggs**
- **1 cup granulated sugar**
- **½ teaspoon vanilla**
- **½ cup butter** *or* **margarine, melted**
- **½ cup unsifted all-purpose flour**
- **⅓ cup Hershey's Cocoa**
- **¼ teaspoon baking powder**
- **¼ teaspoon salt**
- **½ cup chopped nuts, optional**

Beat eggs in small bowl. Gradually add sugar and vanilla; beat well. Blend in melted butter *or* margarine. In a separate bowl combine flour, cocoa, baking powder, and salt. Gradually blend flour mixture into egg mixture until thoroughly blended. Stir in nuts. Spread in a greased, 8-inch square baking pan. Bake at 350° for 30 to 35 minutes or until brownie begins to pull away from edges of pan. Cool in pan. Frost, if desired. Cut into squares.

Peanut Butter Chip Brownies

Makes 16.

- **⅓ cup butter** *or* **margarine**
- **¾ cup granulated sugar**
- **¼ cup light corn syrup**
- **2 teaspoons vanilla**
- **2 eggs**
- **½ cup unsifted all-purpose flour**
- **⅓ cup Hershey's Cocoa**
- **½ teaspoon salt**
- **1 cup Reese's Peanut Butter Chips**

Cream butter *or* margarine and sugar in large bowl. Blend in corn syrup and vanilla. Add eggs, 1 at a time, beating well after each addition. In a separate bowl combine flour, cocoa, and salt; gradually add to creamed mixture. Stir in peanut butter chips. Pour into a greased 8-inch square baking pan. Bake at 350° for 30 to 35 minutes or until brownie begins to pull away from edges of pan. Cool in pan. Frost, if desired. Cut into squares.

Honey Brownies

Makes 16.

- **⅓ cup butter** *or* **margarine**
- **¾ cup granulated sugar**
- **⅓ cup honey**
- **2 teaspoons vanilla**
- **2 eggs**
- **½ cup unsifted all-purpose flour**
- **⅓ cup Hershey's Cocoa**
- **½ teaspoon salt**
- **1 cup chopped nuts**

Cream butter *or* margarine and sugar in a small bowl. Blend in honey and vanilla. Add eggs; beat well. In a separate bowl combine flour, cocoa, and salt. Gradually add to creamed mixture. Stir in nuts. Spread in a greased, 9-inch square baking pan. Bake at 350° for 25 to 30 minutes or until brownie begins to pull away from edges of pan. Cool in pan. Frost, if desired. Cut into squares.

Hi-Protein Energy Bar

Makes 18 bars.

- ½ cup butter *or* margarine
- 1⅓ cups packed brown sugar
- 2 eggs
- 1 teaspoon vanilla
- ⅓ cup Hershey's Cocoa
- ¼ cup milk
- ¼ cup nonfat dry milk crystals
- ¼ cup wheat germ
- 1 cup unsifted whole wheat flour
- ½ teaspoon baking powder
- ¼ teaspoon baking soda
- 2 cups (12-ounce package) Reese's Peanut Butter Chips
- ½ cup raisins

Cream butter *or* margarine, sugar, eggs, and vanilla in large bowl until light and fluffy. Blend in cocoa and milk; add dry milk crystals, wheat germ, flour, baking powder, and baking soda. Beat until ingredients are thoroughly combined. Fold in peanut butter chips and raisins. Spread mixture evenly in a greased 13 x 9 x 2-inch baking pan. Bake at 350° for 30 to 35 minutes. Cool in pan on a wire rack. Cut into bars.

Peanut Butter Chip Breakfast Bars

Makes approximately 5 dozen.

- ¼ cup butter *or* margarine
- ¼ cup shortening
- 1 cup packed light brown sugar
- 1 egg
- 1 teaspoon vanilla
- 1⅓ cups unsifted all-purpose flour
- ½ teaspoon baking soda
- ½ teaspoon salt
- ½ teaspoon ground cinnamon
- ¼ cup milk
- 1⅔ cups granola *or* natural cereal, crumbled
- 1 cup seedless raisins
- 1 cup flaked coconut
- 2 cups (12-ounce package) Reese's Peanut Butter Chips

Cream butter *or* margarine, shortening, brown sugar, egg, and vanilla in large bowl. In a separate bowl combine flour, baking soda, salt, and cinnamon. Alternately add flour mixture and milk to creamed mixture. Stir in cereal, raisins, coconut, and peanut butter chips. Spread batter evenly in a foil-lined 15½ x 10½ x 1-inch jelly-roll pan. Bake at 350° for 20 to 25 minutes. Cool completely. Invert pan. Peel off foil. Cut into 1 x 2-inch bars.

Peanut Butter Chip and Jelly Bars

Makes 3 dozen.

- 3 cups unsifted all-purpose flour
- 1 cup granulated sugar
- 1½ teaspoons baking powder
- 1 cup butter *or* margarine, softened
- 2 eggs, lightly beaten
- 1 cup grape jelly
- 2 cups (12-ounce package) Reese's Peanut Butter Chips

Combine flour, sugar, and baking powder in a large bowl. Cut in butter *or* margarine until mixture resembles coarse crumbs. Stir in beaten eggs; stir until mixture is smooth. Reserve half of the mixture. Press remaining half of mixture onto the bottom of a greased 13 x 9 x 2-inch baking pan. Spread grape jelly evenly over crust in pan. Sprinkle 1 cup peanut butter chips over jelly. Crumble remaining dough over chips. Bake at 375° for 30 to 35 minutes or until lightly browned. Remove from oven. Immediately sprinkle with remaining 1 cup chips. Cool. Cut into bars.

Cherry-Bright Chocolate Brownies

Makes 16.

- ⅓ cup butter *or* margarine
- ¾ cup granulated sugar
- 2 eggs
- ¼ cup light corn syrup
- 2 tablespoons kirsch *or* other cherry liqueur, *or* 1 teaspoon almond extract
- 1 teaspoon vanilla
- ⅔ cup unsifted all-purpose flour
- ⅓ cup Hershey's Cocoa
- ½ teaspoon salt
- ¼ teaspoon baking powder
- ½ cup chopped, well-drained maraschino cherries
- ⅓ cup chopped, slivered almonds
  Halved maraschino cherries, optional

Cream butter *or* margarine, granulated sugar, and eggs in a small bowl. Blend in corn syrup, kirsch *or* almond extract, and vanilla. In a separate bowl combine flour, cocoa, salt, and baking powder. Gradually add flour mixture to creamed mixture; blend well. Stir in chopped cherries and almonds. Spread in a greased and floured 9-inch square baking pan. Bake at 350° for 25 to 30 minutes or until brownie begins to pull away from edges of pan. Cool in pan. Frost, if desired. Cut into squares. Garnish with additional maraschino cherry halves, if desired.

Pies

Cocoa Chiffon-Cloud Pie

Makes 8 servings.

- 1 9-inch baked pastry shell *or* crumb crust, cooled
- 1 envelope unflavored gelatin
- ¼ cup cold water
- ½ cup granulated sugar
- ½ cup Hershey's Cocoa
- ½ teaspoon salt
- 1¼ cups milk
- 3 egg yolks
- 1 cup heavy cream
- 3 egg whites
  Additional whipped cream, optional

Prepare pie shell; set aside.

Sprinkle gelatin over water in a small bowl; let stand to soften, about 5 minutes. Combine sugar, cocoa, and salt in a small saucepan. Stir in milk and egg yolks. Cook over low heat, stirring constantly, until mixture thickens slightly; do *not* boil. Remove from heat. Add gelatin; stir until dissolved. Chill until syrupy. Whip cream until stiff. Gently fold whipped cream into chocolate mixture. Beat egg whites until stiff, but not dry. Fold egg whites into chocolate mixture. Pour mixture into pie shell. Chill until set. Garnish with additional whipped cream, if desired.

Chocolate Bavarian Cream Pie

Makes 8 servings.

- 1 9-inch baked pastry shell *or* crumb crust, cooled
- 1¾ cups milk
- 1 envelope unflavored gelatin
- ⅔ cup granulated sugar
- 6 tablespoons Hershey's Cocoa
- 1 tablespoon light corn syrup
- 2 tablespoons butter *or* margarine
- ¾ teaspoon vanilla
- 1 cup heavy cream

Prepare pie shell; set aside.

Pour 1 cup of the milk into a saucepan. Sprinkle gelatin over milk. Let stand for 5 minutes to soften gelatin. Combine sugar and cocoa; add to mixture in saucepan. Add corn syrup. Cook and stir over medium heat until mixture comes to a boil. Remove from heat. Add butter *or* margarine; stir until melted. Blend in remaining ¾ cup milk and vanilla. Pour into large bowl. Cool to room temperature. Chill until almost set. Whip cream until stiff. Whip chocolate gelatin on medium speed until smooth. Blend half of the whipped cream into the chocolate on low speed just until smooth. Pour into pie shell. Chill until set. Top with remaining whipped cream.

Chocolate Eggnog Chiffon Pie

Makes 8 servings.

- Chocolate Crumb Crust
- 1 envelope unflavored gelatin
- 1¼ cups milk
- 3 egg yolks, lightly beaten
- ¾ cup granulated sugar, divided
- ¼ teaspoon salt
- 1 cup Hershey's Semi-Sweet Chocolate Mini Chips
- 3 tablespoons rum *or* 1 teaspoon rum extract
- ¼ teaspoon nutmeg
- 3 egg whites
- ½ cup heavy cream
  Additional whipped cream and nutmeg, optional

Prepare crumb crust; set aside to cool.

Sprinkle gelatin over milk in saucepan. Let stand 5 minutes to soften gelatin. Blend in egg yolks, ½ cup of the sugar, and salt. Place over medium heat, stirring constantly, until gelatin dissolves and mixture thickens slightly. Do *not* boil. Remove from heat. Place Mini Chips in a bowl. Add about 1 cup of the gelatin mixture to Mini Chips. Stir until melted. Add remaining gelatin mixture, rum, and nutmeg. Cool to room temperature. Chill until almost set. Remove from refrigerator. Beat 1 minute with mixer until smooth.

Beat egg whites in small bowl until foamy. Gradually add remaining ¼ cup sugar, beating until stiff peaks form. Fold into chocolate mixture.

Whip cream in small bowl until stiff; fold into chocolate mixture. Chill 15 minutes. Mound into pie shell. If desired, garnish with additional whipped cream and sprinkle with nutmeg.

Chocolate Crumb Crust

- 1½ cups vanilla wafer crumbs
- 6 tablespoons Hershey's Cocoa
- ⅓ cup confectioners' sugar
- 6 tablespoons butter *or* margarine, melted

Combine crumbs, cocoa, and sugar in a bowl. Stir in butter *or* margarine. Press mixture onto bottom and sides of a 9-inch pie plate. Bake at 350° for 8 to 10 minutes. Cool.

Chocolate Bavarian Cream Pie, above

Pies

Chocolate-Butterscotch Pie

Makes 8 servings.

      Macaroon-Nut Crust
- ⅔ cup packed light brown sugar
- ¼ cup Hershey's Cocoa
- 3 tablespoons unsifted all-purpose flour
- 2 tablespoons cornstarch
- ½ teaspoon salt
- 2¼ cups milk
- ½ cup light corn syrup
- 3 egg yolks, beaten
- 2 tablespoons butter *or* margarine
- 1 teaspoon vanilla
- Sweetened whipped cream, optional

Prepare Macaroon-Nut Crust; set aside.

Combine sugar, cocoa, flour, cornstarch, and salt in a medium saucepan. Blend in milk, corn syrup, and egg yolks. Cook over medium heat, stirring constantly, until mixture comes to a boil. Boil and stir for 1 minute. Remove from heat. Blend in butter *or* margarine and vanilla. Pour into cooled pie shell. Carefully press plastic wrap directly onto pie filling. Cool to room temperature. Chill. Serve with sweetened whipped cream, if desired.

Macaroon-Nut Crust

- 1¼ cups crisp coconut cookie crumbs
- ½ cup chopped walnuts
- ¼ cup melted butter *or* margarine

Combine all ingredients in a small bowl; blend well. Press firmly into a 9-inch pie plate. Bake at 350° for 8 to 10 minutes; cool.

Chocolate Swirl Ice Cream Pie

Makes 8 to 10 servings.

      Chocolate Cookie Crust
      Chocolate Sauce
- 1½ quarts strawberry, peppermint, *or* coffee ice cream, slightly softened
- Sweetened strawberries, optional

Prepare Chocolate Cookie Crust.

Prepare Chocolate Sauce.

Spread about half of the ice cream into the frozen pie shell. Spoon about ½ cup of the Chocolate Sauce over the ice cream. Top with remaining ice cream. Drizzle on ¼ cup of the Chocolate Sauce. Freeze until firm. Cover with plastic wrap or aluminum foil. Serve with remaining Chocolate Sauce. Garnish with sweetened strawberries, if desired.

Chocolate Cookie Crust

- 1½ cups chocolate wafer cookie crumbs
- ⅓ cup butter *or* margarine, melted

Combine chocolate cookie crumbs and melted butter *or* margarine in a 9-inch pie plate. Press firmly against the bottom and sides. Bake at 350° for 8 to 10 minutes. Cool; freeze.

Chocolate Sauce

Makes approximately 1 cup.

- ¼ cup granulated sugar
- 2 tablespoons unsifted all-purpose flour
- 2 tablespoons milk
- 1 egg, well beaten
- ½ cup (5.5-ounce can) Hershey's Chocolate Flavored Syrup
- ¼ cup butter *or* margarine
- ½ teaspoon vanilla

Mix sugar and flour in a small saucepan. Blend in milk, egg, and chocolate syrup. Cook over low heat, stirring constantly, until mixture comes to a boil. Boil and stir 1 minute. Remove from heat. Blend in butter *or* margarine and vanilla. Cool.

Chocolate Peppermint Whirlaway Pie

Makes 8 to 10 servings.

      Graham Cracker Crust (Recipe on page 21)
- 36 large marshmallows *or* 3½ cups miniature marshmallows
- ¾ cup milk
- 1½ teaspoons vanilla
- ⅛ teaspoon pure mint *or* peppermint extract
- Chocolate Sauce (Recipe above)
- ⅛ teaspoon red food color
- 3½ cups (1 8-ounce container) frozen nondairy whipped topping, thawed

Prepare piecrust; set aside. Melt marshmallows with milk in the top of a double boiler over hot, *not* boiling, water; stir until smooth. Cool slightly. Stir in vanilla and extract. Chill, stirring occasionally, until mixture mounds when dropped from a spoon. Prepare Chocolate Sauce; cool. Set aside ½ cup. Fold marshmallow mixture and food color into whipped topping in a small bowl. Alternately layer marshmallow mixture with Chocolate Sauce in crumb crust. Swirl with a rubber spatula to create a marbled effect. Cover; freeze several hours or overnight. Serve with reserved sauce.

Milk Chocolate Pie

Makes 8 servings.

    Graham Cracker Crust
    1 (½ pound) Hershey's Milk Chocolate Bar
    ¼ cup milk
    3½ cups (1 8-ounce container) frozen nondairy
        whipped topping, thawed or whipped cream
        Hershey's Semi-Sweet Chocolate Mini Chips

Prepare Graham Cracker Crust; set aside. Break chocolate bar into pieces. Melt chocolate with milk in the top of double boiler over hot, *not* boiling, water. Cool completely. Fold whipped topping *or* whipped cream into cooled chocolate. Pour into crust. Garnish with Mini Chips. Cover; chill several hours until firm. Can also be frozen.

Graham Cracker Crust

    1¼ cups graham cracker crumbs
    ¼ cup granulated sugar
    ¼ cup butter or margarine, melted

Combine crumbs, sugar, and melted butter *or* margarine in a medium bowl. Blend thoroughly with a fork or pastry blender. Press mixture into the bottom and sides of a 9-inch pie plate. Bake at 350° for 8 to 10 minutes. Cool.

Chocolate Peanut Butter Pie

Makes 8 servings.

    Peanut Butter Chip Crust
    1 cup Reese's Peanut Butter Chips
    1 cup Hershey's Semi-Sweet Chocolate Mini Chips
    1 envelope unflavored gelatin
    ½ cup granulated sugar
    1¾ cups milk
    2 egg yolks, lightly beaten
    1 teaspoon vanilla
    2 egg whites
    1 tablespoon granulated sugar
    Whipped cream, optional
    Chocolate shavings or Reese's Peanut Butter
        Chips, optional

Prepare Peanut Butter Chip Crust; set aside. Place peanut butter chips into one bowl and Mini Chips into a second bowl; set aside. Combine gelatin and ½ cup sugar in a saucepan. Add milk and egg yolks. Cook over medium heat, stirring constantly, until gelatin is dissolved and mixture lightly coats a spoon. Do *not* boil. Remove from heat. Stir in vanilla. Slowly pour 1 cup of the gelatin mixture into the bowl containing the chocolate; stir until melted. Gradually add remaining hot mixture, ½ cup at a time, to the peanut butter chips; stir until melted. Chill both mixtures until partially set. Pour chocolate into prepared pie shell. Beat egg whites with the 1 tablespoon sugar. Fold egg whites into peanut butter mixture. Pour over chocolate layer. Chill thoroughly before serving. Garnish with whipped cream and chocolate shavings or additional peanut butter chips, if desired.

Peanut Butter Chip Crust

    ¾ cup Reese's Peanut Butter Chips
    1 cup vanilla wafers or graham cracker crumbs
    2 tablespoons granulated sugar
    5 tablespoons butter or margarine,
        melted and cooled

Chop peanut butter chips with a nut chopper or blender. Add crushed chips to cookie crumbs and sugar. Drizzle on melted butter *or* margarine. Blend thoroughly. Press mixture into bottom and sides of a 9-inch pie plate. Chill.

Chocolate Amaretto Pie

Makes 8 servings.

    Graham Cracker Crust (Recipe on this page)
    ⅓ cup Hershey's Cocoa
    1 cup granulated sugar
    ⅓ cup cornstarch
    ¼ teaspoon salt
    2¾ cups milk
    3 tablespoons Amaretto
    2 tablespoons butter or margarine
    1 teaspoon vanilla
    Sliced almonds, optional

Prepare piecrust; set aside.

Combine cocoa, sugar, cornstarch, and salt in a medium saucepan. Gradually blend in milk; stir until smooth. Cook over medium heat, stirring constantly, until mixture comes to a boil; boil and stir 1 minute. Remove from heat. Blend in Amaretto, butter *or* margarine, and vanilla. Pour into piecrust. Chill until firm. Just before serving, pipe on Amaretto Whipped Cream. Garnish with sliced almonds, if desired.

Amaretto Whipped Cream

Makes approximately 1 cup.

    ½ cup heavy cream
    2 tablespoons confectioners' sugar
    1 to 2 teaspoons Amaretto

Whip cream, sugar, and Amaretto until stiff.

Pies

Velvety Chocolate Cream Pie

Makes 8 servings.

    1 9-inch baked pastry shell or crumb crust, cooled
    ⅓ cup Hershey's Cocoa
    1¼ cups granulated sugar
    ⅓ cup cornstarch
    ¼ teaspoon salt
    3 cups milk
    3 tablespoons butter or margarine
    1½ teaspoons vanilla
      Sweetened whipped cream or nondairy whipped
      topping, optional
      Chocolate curls, optional

Prepare pie shell; set aside.

Combine cocoa, sugar, cornstarch, and salt in a medium saucepan. Blend in milk until smooth. Cook and stir over medium heat until mixture comes to a boil. Boil and stir for 3 minutes. Remove from heat. Blend in butter or margarine and vanilla. Pour into pie shell. Carefully press plastic wrap directly onto pie filling. Chill 3 to 4 hours. Serve with sweetened whipped cream or whipped topping and chocolate curls, if desired.

Variations

Mocha: Add 2 teaspoons dry instant coffee to dry ingredients.

Rum: Omit vanilla. Add 3 to 4 tablespoons light rum.

Chocolate Coconut Cream Pie

Makes 8 servings.

    1 9-inch baked pastry shell or crumb crust, cooled
    ⅔ cup granulated sugar
    ⅓ cup cornstarch
    ¼ teaspoon salt
    3 cups milk
    3 egg yolks, lightly beaten
    1 tablespoon butter
    2 teaspoons vanilla
    ½ cup flaked coconut
    3 tablespoons Hershey's Cocoa
    3 tablespoons granulated sugar
    2 tablespoons milk
    3 egg whites
    ¼ teaspoon cream of tartar
    6 tablespoons granulated sugar

Prepare pie shell; set aside.

Combine the ⅔ cup sugar, cornstarch, salt, and 3 cups milk in a medium saucepan. Blend in egg yolks. Stir constantly over medium heat until mixture comes to a boil. Boil and stir for 1 minute. Remove from heat. Stir in butter and vanilla. Pour 1½ cups of the cooked mixture into a small bowl. Stir in coconut. Set aside.

Combine cocoa, the 3 tablespoons sugar, and the 2 tablespoons milk in a small bowl. Blend cocoa mixture into remaining mixture in saucepan. Pour 1 cup of the chocolate mixture into the pie shell. Spread coconut mixture over chocolate. Top with remaining chocolate mixture; spread evenly. Prepare meringue by beating egg whites with cream of tartar until foamy. Gradually add the 6 tablespoons sugar; beat until stiff peaks form. Spread meringue over hot pie filling, carefully sealing to edge of crust. Bake at 350° for 8 to 10 minutes or until lightly browned. Cool to room temperature; chill several hours.

Chocolate Banana Cream Pie

Makes 8 servings.

    1 9-inch baked pastry shell or crumb crust, cooled
    2 ounces Hershey's Unsweetened Baking Chocolate
    2½ cups milk
    1 cup granulated sugar
    5 tablespoons cornstarch
    ½ teaspoon salt
    3 egg yolks, lightly beaten
    1 tablespoon butter
    1 teaspoon vanilla
    2 medium bananas, sliced
    1 cup nondairy whipped topping or
      whipped cream, optional

Prepare piecrust; set aside.

Place baking chocolate and 1½ cups of the milk in top of double boiler over simmering water; heat and stir until chocolate is melted. In a separate bowl combine sugar, cornstarch, and salt; blend in remaining 1 cup milk. Gradually add to chocolate mixture, stirring constantly. Immediately add egg yolks. Cook until mixture thickens, stirring constantly. Cook and stir 5 minutes longer. Remove from heat. Add butter and vanilla. Pour into a bowl. Press plastic wrap directly onto filling. Cool. Spread a small amount of filling over the bottom of the pie shell. Arrange a layer of banana slices on top of filling. Spread on remaining filling. Press plastic wrap directly onto filling. Chill. Serve garnished with whipped topping or whipped cream, if desired.

Cakes

Cocoa Cake Roll

Makes 10 to 12 servings.

      3 egg yolks
    ½ cup granulated sugar
    ½ cup unsifted all-purpose flour
    ⅓ cup Hershey's Cocoa
    ⅓ cup granulated sugar
    ½ teaspoon baking soda
    ¼ teaspoon salt
    ⅓ cup water
      1 teaspoon vanilla
      3 egg whites
      1 tablespoon granulated sugar
         Peanut Butter Whipped Cream Filling
         Chocolate Glaze

Line a 15½ x 10½ x 1-inch jelly-roll pan with aluminum foil; grease foil generously. Beat egg yolks in a small bowl on high speed about 3 minutes; gradually add ½ cup sugar. Continue beating for 2 minutes. In a separate bowl combine flour, cocoa, ⅓ cup sugar, baking soda, and salt; add alternately with water and vanilla on low speed just until batter is smooth. Beat egg whites until foamy; add 1 tablespoon sugar and beat until stiff peaks form. Carefully fold beaten egg whites into chocolate mixture. Spread batter evenly into prepared pan. Bake at 375° for 15 to 18 minutes or until top springs back when touched lightly. Invert onto slightly dampened towel; carefully remove foil. Immediately roll cake and towel together from narrow end. Let stand 1 minute. Unroll and remove towel; reroll cake. Cool completely on a wire rack. Prepare Peanut Butter Whipped Cream Filling.

Unroll cake and spread with filling; reroll. Garnish with additional whipped cream and Chocolate Glaze. Chill about 1 hour before serving.

Peanut Butter Whipped Cream Filling

      1 cup Reese's Peanut Butter Chips
    ⅓ cup milk
    1½ cups miniature marshmallows or
         15 large marshmallows
      1 cup heavy cream
    ½ teaspoon vanilla

Place peanut butter chips, milk, and marshmallows in top of double boiler over simmering water. Stir until marshmallows and chips are completely melted; cool to lukewarm. Whip heavy cream until stiff; fold in vanilla and peanut butter mixture.

Chocolate Glaze

      2 tablespoons butter or margarine
      2 tablespoons Hershey's Cocoa
      2 tablespoons water
      1 cup confectioners' sugar
    ½ teaspoon vanilla

Melt butter or margarine in a small saucepan over low heat; add cocoa and water, stirring constantly, until mixture thickens. Do *not* boil. Remove from heat; cool slightly. (Cool completely for a thicker, frosting-type topping.) Blend in confectioners' sugar and vanilla.

5-Way Chocolate Cake

Makes 8 to 10 servings.

    ½ cup butter or margarine
    ½ cup shortening
    2¼ cups granulated sugar
      2 eggs
      1 teaspoon vanilla
    ⅔ cup Hershey's Cocoa
    2½ cups unsifted all-purpose flour
    1½ teaspoons baking soda
    ½ teaspoon baking powder
      1 teaspoon salt
      2 cups buttermilk

Cream butter or margarine, shortening, and sugar in a large bowl until light and fluffy. Add eggs and vanilla; beat well. In a separate bowl combine cocoa, flour, baking soda, baking powder, and salt; add alternately with buttermilk to creamed mixture. Pour into well-greased and floured pans. Bake at 350° as follows: three 8-inch round cake pans for 30 to 35 minutes; one 13 x 9 x 2-inch pan for 55 to 65 minutes; one 10-inch tube or Bundt pan for 55 to 65 minutes; two 9 x 5 x 3-inch loaf pans for 50 to 60 minutes. For 3½ dozen cupcakes (2½ inches in diameter), bake 20 to 25 minutes at 375°.

Orange-Kissed Chocolate Cupcakes

Makes 24.

    ¾ cup shortening
 1¼ cups granulated sugar
    2 eggs
    1 teaspoon vanilla
 1¾ cups unsifted all-purpose flour
    ½ cup Hershey's Cocoa
    1 teaspoon baking soda
    ½ teaspoon salt
    1 cup milk
      Orange or Vanilla Cream Filling
    1 6-ounce package (about 24) Hershey's Milk
      Chocolate Kisses

Cream shortening and sugar in large bowl. Add eggs and vanilla; blend well. In a separate bowl combine flour, cocoa, baking soda, and salt; add alternately with milk to creamed mixture. Fill 24 paper-lined 2½-inch muffin cups two-thirds full with batter. Bake at 375° for 20 to 25 minutes or until cake tester inserted comes out clean. Cool completely.

Prepare Orange or Vanilla Cream Filling. Cut a 1½-inch cone from top of cupcake. Fill cavity with filling; replace cone. Swirl filling over top. Top with *unwrapped* Chocolate Kiss.

Orange Cream Filling

Makes approximately 3 cups.

    ¼ cup unsifted all-purpose flour
    ½ cup milk
    ¼ cup butter or margarine
    ¼ cup shortening
    1 tablespoon finely grated orange peel
    2 teaspoons orange juice
    ¼ teaspoon salt
    4 cups confectioners' sugar
      Red and yellow food color, optional

Combine flour and milk in a small saucepan. Cook, stirring constantly, until mixture thickens and just begins to boil. Remove from heat. Chill thoroughly.

Cream butter or margarine and shortening in large bowl. Add orange peel, orange juice, and salt; blend in chilled flour mixture. Gradually add confectioners' sugar, beating to spreading consistency. Stir in food color, if desired.

Variation

Vanilla Cream Filling: Substitute 2 teaspoons vanilla for orange juice and grated peel. Omit food color.

Cocoa-Lite Angel Food Cake

Makes 12 to 14 servings.

    1 14½-ounce box Angel Food Cake mix
    ⅓ cup Hershey's Cocoa
      Mocha Chiffon Filling

Prepare egg white mixture as directed on package. Pour contents of cake flour mixture into small bowl. Stir cocoa into cake flour mixture until well blended. Blend cocoa-cake flour mixture gradually into beaten egg whites. Mix at low speed and scrape bowl often until dry mix disappears, about 1 minute. Pour batter into two ungreased 9 x 5 x 3-inch loaf pans or a 10-inch tube pan. Cut through batter with knife or spatula to remove large air bubbles. Bake at 375° for 30 to 40 minutes or until top crust is golden brown, firm, and looks dry. Do *not* underbake. Cool in pan, inverted on cooling rack or hanging upside down on funnel or bottle. When completely cool, slice loaf or ring into 3 thin layers horizontally. Spread each layer generously with ¾ cup Mocha Chiffon Filling, reserving ¼ cup for garnish or frosting top.

Mocha Chiffon Filling

Makes 2 cups.

    1 envelope dry whipped topping mix
    ½ cup cold low-fat or skim milk
    1 teaspoon instant coffee granules
    2 teaspoons Hershey's Cocoa
    1 teaspoon vanilla

Combine ingredients in deep, narrow-bottom bowl at low speed until blended. Whip on high speed until soft peaks form. Whip 2 minutes longer or until topping is light and fluffy.

Chocolate Fudge Cake

Makes 10 to 12 servings.

- ½ cup butter *or* margarine, softened
- ½ cup shortening
- 2 cups granulated sugar
- 2 eggs
- 1 teaspoon vanilla
- 2¼ cups unsifted all-purpose flour
- ½ cup Hershey's Cocoa
- 1¼ teaspoons baking soda
- ½ teaspoon salt
- 1⅓ cups water

Cream butter *or* margarine, shortening, and sugar in large bowl. Add eggs and vanilla; blend thoroughly. In a separate bowl combine flour, cocoa, baking soda, and salt; add alternately with water to creamed mixture. Pour into two greased and floured 9-inch round cake pans or two 8-inch square cake pans. Bake at 350° for 35 to 40 minutes for 9-inch layers; 40 to 45 minutes for 8-inch layers or until cake tester inserted comes out clean. Cool 10 minutes; remove from pans. Cool completely on wire racks; frost.

Chocolate Chiffon Peanut Butter Cake

Makes 10 to 12 servings.

- 1½ cups unsifted cake flour
- 1¾ cups granulated sugar
- ⅔ cup Hershey's Cocoa
- 2 teaspoons baking powder
- ½ teaspoon baking soda
- 1 teaspoon salt
- ½ cup vegetable oil
- 7 eggs, separated
- ¾ cup cold water
- 2 teaspoons vanilla
- ½ teaspoon cream of tartar
- ¼ cup granulated sugar
- Peanut Butter Whipped Cream

Combine flour, 1¾ cups sugar, cocoa, baking powder, baking soda, and salt in a large bowl. Make a well in mixture; add oil, egg yolks, water, and vanilla. Beat with a wooden spoon until smooth.

Beat egg whites and cream of tartar in large bowl until frothy; gradually add ¼ cup sugar and beat until stiff peaks form.

Gradually pour chocolate batter over beaten egg whites, gently folding just until blended. Pour

into ungreased 10-inch tube pan. Bake at 325° for 1 hour and 20 to 30 minutes or until done (cake springs back when lightly touched). Invert cake over funnel or bottle until completely cool. Loosen cake with spatula. Invert on serving plate. Prepare Peanut Butter Whipped Cream; frost. Garnish as desired.

Peanut Butter Whipped Cream

- 1 cup Reese's Peanut Butter Chips
- ⅓ cup milk
- 1½ cups miniature marshmallows *or* 15 large marshmallows
- 1 cup heavy cream
- ½ teaspoon vanilla

Place peanut butter chips, milk, and marshmallows in top of double boiler over simmering water. Stir until marshmallows and chips are completely melted; cool to lukewarm. Whip heavy cream until stiff; fold in vanilla and peanut butter mixture.

Red Velvet Cocoa Cake

Makes 10 to 12 servings.

- ½ cup butter *or* margarine
- 1½ cups granulated sugar
- 1 teaspoon vanilla
- 2 eggs
- 1 tablespoon red food color
- 2 cups unsifted all-purpose flour
- ¼ cup Hershey's Cocoa
- 1 teaspoon salt
- 1 cup buttermilk *or* sour milk*
- 1½ teaspoons baking soda
- 1 tablespoon vinegar
- Fluffy Vanilla Frosting (See recipe on page 37)

Cream butter *or* margarine, sugar, and vanilla in large bowl. Add eggs and food color; blend thoroughly. In separate bowl combine flour, cocoa, and salt; add alternately with buttermilk *or* sour milk to creamed mixture. Stir baking soda into vinegar; fold carefully into batter (do *not* beat). Pour into two greased and floured 9-inch round cake pans. Bake at 350° for 30 to 35 minutes or until cake tester inserted comes out clean. Cool 10 minutes; remove from pans. Cool completely on wire racks; frost with Fluffy Vanilla Frosting.

To Sour Milk: Use 1 tablespoon vinegar plus milk to equal 1 cup.

Cakes

Mini Chip Petits Fours

Makes approximately 5½ dozen.

 ⅔ cup butter *or* margarine
1⅓ cups granulated sugar
 1 teaspoon vanilla
 2 eggs
 2 cups unsifted all-purpose flour
1¼ teaspoons baking powder
 ¼ teaspoon salt
 ⅔ cup milk
 1 cup Hershey's Semi-Sweet Chocolate Mini Chips
   Chocolate Petits Fours Glaze

Line a 15½ x 10½ x 1-inch jelly-roll pan with aluminum foil; grease foil.

Cream butter *or* margarine, sugar, and vanilla in large bowl until light and fluffy. Add eggs, beating well. In a separate bowl combine flour, baking powder, and salt; add alternately with milk to creamed mixture, beating just until smooth. Stir in Mini Chips. Pour batter into prepared pan. Bake at 350° for 20 to 25 minutes or until cake tester inserted comes out clean. Cool 10 minutes; remove from pan. Remove foil; cool completely. Cut cake into hearts, diamonds, circles, or squares (approximately 1½-inch shapes). Place cake pieces on a wire rack with waxed paper or cookie sheet below to catch drips. Cover until ready to glaze.

Prepare Chocolate Petits Fours Glaze. Frost by spooning chocolate glaze over cake pieces so entire piece is covered. Allow glaze to set. Decorate with Mini Chips and/or candied fruit pieces, or pipe decorations with tubes of glossy decorating gels or frosting.

Note: Cake can also be baked in a greased and floured 9 x 5 x 3-inch loaf pan at 350° for 55 to 60 minutes. Cover with Chocolate Petits Fours Glaze and garnish with Mini Chips.

Chocolate Petits Fours Glaze

 ⅓ cup granulated sugar
 3 tablespoons water
 1 cup Hershey's Semi-Sweet Chocolate Mini Chips
 3 tablespoons marshmallow creme
 1 to 2 tablespoons hot water

Combine sugar and 3 tablespoons water in a small saucepan; bring to a boil. Remove from heat and immediately add Mini Chips; stir until melted. Blend in marshmallow creme and enough hot water until glaze is of pouring consistency. Remelt the drippings over hot water as additional glaze is needed.

Sour Cream Chocolate Cake

Makes 10 to 12 servings.

 3 ounces Hershey's Unsweetened Baking Chocolate
 ½ cup butter *or* margarine
 1 cup boiling water
 2 cups packed light brown sugar
 2 cups unsifted all-purpose flour
1½ teaspoons baking soda
 1 teaspoon salt
 2 eggs
 ½ cup sour cream
 1 teaspoon vanilla

Combine baking chocolate, butter *or* margarine, and boiling water in a small bowl; stir until chocolate and butter *or* margarine are melted. Combine brown sugar, flour, baking soda, and salt in large bowl. Gradually add chocolate mixture; blend well. Add eggs, sour cream, and vanilla; beat one minute at medium speed. Pour into a greased and floured 13 x 9 x 2-inch pan. Bake at 350° for 35 minutes or until cake tester inserted comes out clean.

Vermont Cocoa Cake

Makes 10 to 12 servings.

 ½ cup Hershey's Cocoa
 ½ cup boiling water
 ¼ cup butter *or* margarine
 ¼ cup shortening
 2 cups granulated sugar
 ⅛ teaspoon salt
 1 teaspoon vanilla
 2 eggs
1½ teaspoons baking soda
 1 cup buttermilk *or* sour milk*
1¾ cups unsifted all-purpose flour
 3 tablespoons buttermilk *or* sour milk**
 1 teaspoon imitation maple flavor
 ⅓ cup chopped walnuts

Stir together cocoa and boiling water in small bowl until smooth; set aside. Cream butter *or* margarine, shortening, sugar, salt, and vanilla in a large bowl. Add eggs; beat well. Stir baking soda into 1 cup buttermilk *or* sour milk; add alternately with flour to creamed mixture.

Measure 1⅔ cups batter into a small bowl. Stir in 3 tablespoons buttermilk *or* sour milk, maple flavor, and nuts; pour into a greased and waxed paper-lined 8- or 9-inch layer pan. Blend cocoa mixture into remaining batter; pour into two greased and waxed paper-lined 8- or 9-inch round cake pans. Bake at 350° for 30 to 35 minutes for 8-inch layers; 25 to 30 minutes for 9-inch layers or until cake tester inserted comes out clean. Cool 5 minutes; remove from pans. Cool completely on wire racks. Fill and frost, placing Maple-Nut layer between cocoa layers.

Variation

Orange-Nut: Stir ⅛ teaspoon baking soda into the 3 tablespoons buttermilk *or* sour milk before adding to 1⅔ cups batter. Substitute ½ to ¾ teaspoon grated orange peel for maple flavor. Prepare recipe as above.

To Sour Milk: Use 1 tablespoon vinegar plus milk to equal 1 cup.

**To Sour Milk:* Use ½ teaspoon vinegar plus milk to equal 3 tablespoons.

Chocolate Syrup Swirl Cake

Makes 12 to 14 servings.

    1 cup butter *or* margarine
    2 cups granulated sugar
    3 eggs
    2 teaspoons vanilla
 2¾ cups unsifted all-purpose flour
    1 teaspoon baking soda
   ½ teaspoon salt
    1 cup buttermilk *or* sour milk*
    1 cup Hershey's Chocolate Flavored Syrup
   ¼ teaspoon baking soda
    1 cup flaked coconut, optional
      Mini Chip-Marshmallow Glaze

Cream butter *or* margarine and sugar in large bowl; blend in eggs and vanilla. In a separate bowl combine flour, 1 teaspoon baking soda, and salt; add alternately with buttermilk *or* sour milk to creamed mixture. Combine chocolate syrup and ¼ teaspoon baking soda; blend into 2 cups batter. Add coconut, if desired, to remaining batter and pour into a greased and floured 12-cup Bundt pan or 10-inch tube pan. Pour chocolate batter over vanilla batter in pan; do *not* mix. Bake at 350° about 1 hour and 10 minutes. Cool 15 minutes; remove from pan. Cool completely on wire rack; drizzle with Mini Chip-Marshmallow Glaze.

To Sour Milk: Use 1 tablespoon vinegar plus milk to equal 1 cup.

Cocoa Snowballs

Makes 30.

    3 eggs
 1½ cups granulated sugar
   ½ cup Hershey's Cocoa
   ¾ cup milk
   ¼ cup butter *or* margarine
    1 teaspoon vanilla
   ½ teaspoon salt
 1½ cups unsifted all-purpose flour
   ½ teaspoon baking soda
    2 7.2-ounce packages fluffy white frosting mix
 2⅔ cups flaked coconut

Beat eggs until thick and lemon colored in a small bowl. Gradually beat in ½ cup sugar. Combine remaining 1 cup sugar and cocoa in saucepan. Add milk and butter *or* margarine; cook and stir constantly until sugar is dissolved and butter *or* margarine is melted. Remove from heat; add vanilla and salt. Pour egg mixture into a large bowl. In a separate bowl combine flour and baking soda; fold alternately with chocolate mixture into egg mixture just until blended. Fill 30 paper-lined 2½-inch muffin cups about one-half full with batter. Bake at 325° for 20 to 25 minutes or until cake tester inserted comes out clean. Cool completely. Prepare frosting mix according to package directions. Remove cupcake papers. Frost top, bottom, and sides of each cupcake; roll in coconut. Let stand at room temperature until frosting is firm.

Mini Chip-Marshmallow Glaze

Makes approximately 1 cup

   ⅓ cup granulated sugar
    3 tablespoons water
    1 cup Hershey's Semi-Sweet Chocolate Mini Chips
    3 tablespoons marshmallow creme
    1 to 2 tablespoons hot water

Combine sugar and the 3 tablespoons of water in a small saucepan. Bring to a boil. Remove from heat. Immediately add Mini Chips; stir until melted. Blend in marshmallow creme. Add hot water, 1 teaspoon at a time, stirring until glaze is desired consistency.

Holiday Chocolate Cake

Makes 10 to 12 servings.

  2 cups granulated sugar
1¾ cups unsifted all-purpose flour
  ¾ cup Hershey's Cocoa
  2 teaspoons baking soda
  1 teaspoon baking powder
  1 teaspoon salt
  2 eggs
  1 cup buttermilk *or* sour milk*
  1 cup strong black coffee *or* 2 teaspoons instant
    coffee dissolved in 1 cup hot water
  ½ cup vegetable oil
  2 teaspoons vanilla
    Ricotta Cheese Filling
    Chocolate Whipped Cream Frosting

Combine sugar, flour, cocoa, baking soda, baking powder, and salt in large bowl. Add eggs, buttermilk *or* sour milk, coffee, oil, and vanilla; beat at medium speed for 2 minutes (batter will be thin). Pour into two greased and floured 9-inch round cake pans. Bake at 350° for 30 to 35 minutes or until cake tester inserted comes out clean. Cool 10 minutes; remove from pans. Cool completely on wire racks. Slice cake layers in half horizontally. Place bottom slice on serving plate; top with one-third of Ricotta Cheese Filling. Alternate cake layers and filling ending with cake on top. Frost with Chocolate Whipped Cream.

To Sour Milk: Use 1 tablespoon vinegar plus milk to equal 1 cup.

Ricotta Cheese Filling

1¾ cups (15 ounces) ricotta cheese*
  ¼ cup granulated sugar
  3 tablespoons Grand Marnier *or* orange-flavored
    liqueur *or* orange juice concentrate, undiluted
  ¼ cup candied red *or* green cherries,
    coarsely chopped
  ⅓ cup Hershey's Semi-Sweet Chocolate Mini Chips

Combine ricotta cheese, sugar, and liqueur in small bowl; beat until smooth. Fold in candied fruit and Mini Chips.

*If ricotta cheese is unavailable, substitute 1 cup heavy cream. Whip with sugar and liqueur until stiff.

Chocolate Whipped Cream

Makes approximately 2½ cups.

  ⅓ cup confectioners' sugar
  2 tablespoons Hershey's Cocoa
  1 cup heavy cream
  1 teaspoon vanilla

Combine confectioners' sugar and cocoa in small bowl. Add cream and vanilla; beat until stiff.

Orange-Frosted Cocoa Bundt Cake

Makes 12 to 14 servings.

  ¾ cup butter *or* margarine
1⅔ cups granulated sugar
  2 eggs
  1 teaspoon vanilla
  ¾ cup sour cream
  2 cups unsifted all-purpose flour
  ⅔ cup Hershey's Cocoa
  ½ teaspoon salt
  2 teaspoons baking soda
  1 cup buttermilk *or* sour milk*
    Orange *or* Vanilla Frosting

Cream butter *or* margarine, sugar, eggs, and vanilla in large bowl; blend in sour cream. In a separate bowl combine flour, cocoa, and salt. Stir baking soda into buttermilk *or* sour milk; add alternately with dry ingredients to creamed mixture. Beat 2 minutes at medium speed. Pour batter into greased and floured 9-cup or 12-cup Bundt pan. Bake at 350° for 45 to 50 minutes or until cake tester inserted comes out clean. Cool 10 minutes; remove from pan. Cool completely on a wire rack. Frost with Orange *or* Vanilla Frosting.

Orange Frosting

  1 cup confectioners' sugar
  2 tablespoons butter *or* margarine, melted
1½ tablespoons orange juice
  ½ teaspoon vanilla
  ¼ teaspoon grated orange peel

Combine all ingredients in small bowl; beat until smooth.

Variation

Vanilla Frosting: Substitute 1½ tablespoons water for orange juice and omit orange peel. Prepare as above.

To Sour Milk: Use 1 tablespoon vinegar plus milk to equal 1 cup.

Cocoa Cake Roll, 24
Holiday Chocolate Cake, above

Index

CAKES

COOKIES

PIES

B
C 3
D 4
E 5
F 6
G 7
    8
H 9
I 0
J